WHERE'S the ELF?
ACTIVITY BOOK

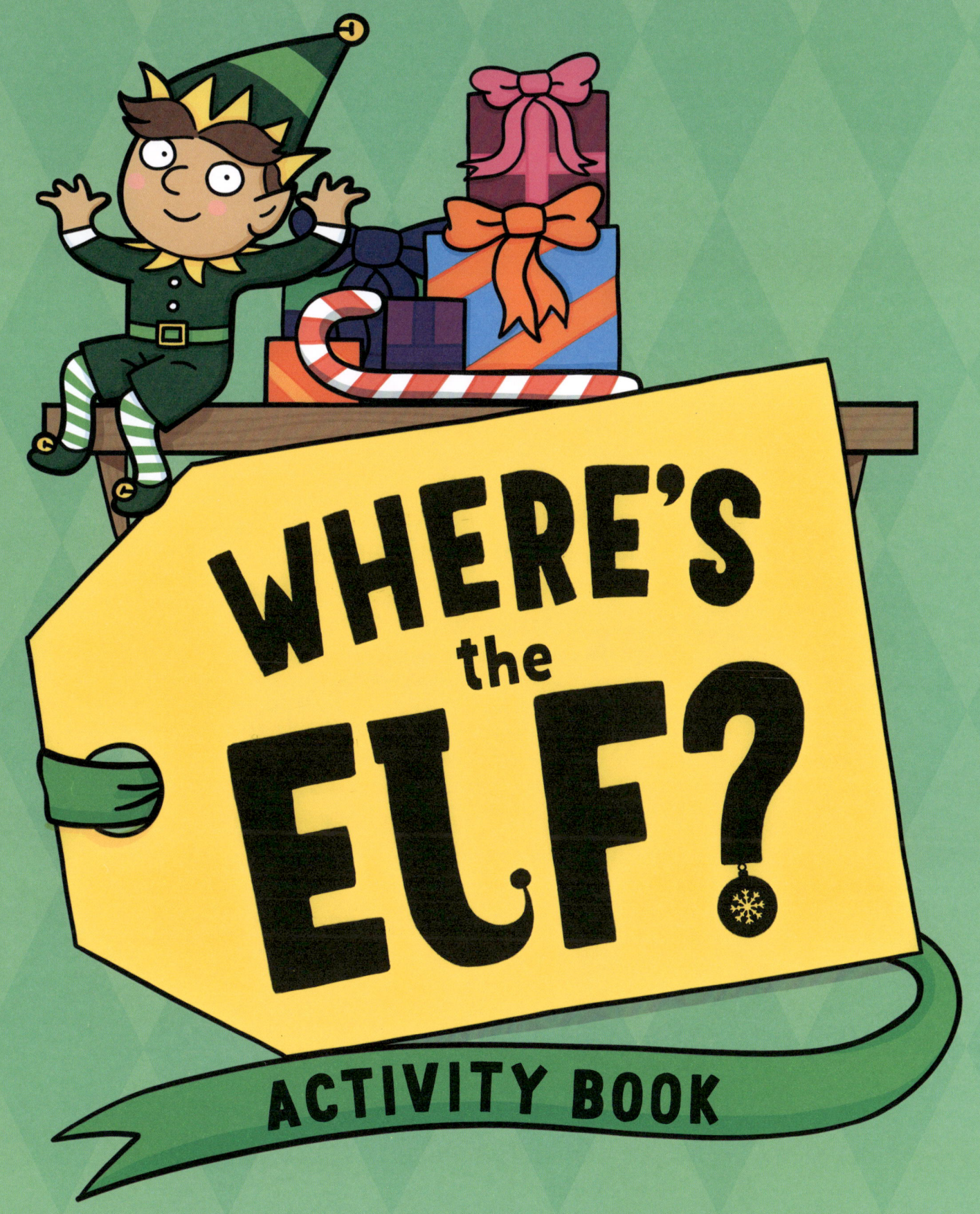

INTRODUCTION

Santa and his merry team of Christmas elves are ready for a festive adventure! This book is packed with all sorts of seasonal challenges, from jolly mazes and Christmassy spot-the-differences to cheerful quizzes and merry puzzles.

Team up with Santa and the elves to spread holiday cheer and complete each activity in time for the big day. Follow the instructions at the top of each page and enjoy hours of festive fun.

So, grab your pens or pencils and get ready for a holly jolly Christmas adventure!

Marching Shadows

Only one of the silhouettes below perfectly matches the Nutcracker. Can you tell which one?

Wonderful Wreaths!

The elves have been busy making lots of beautiful Christmas wreaths! How many can you find in the jumble below?

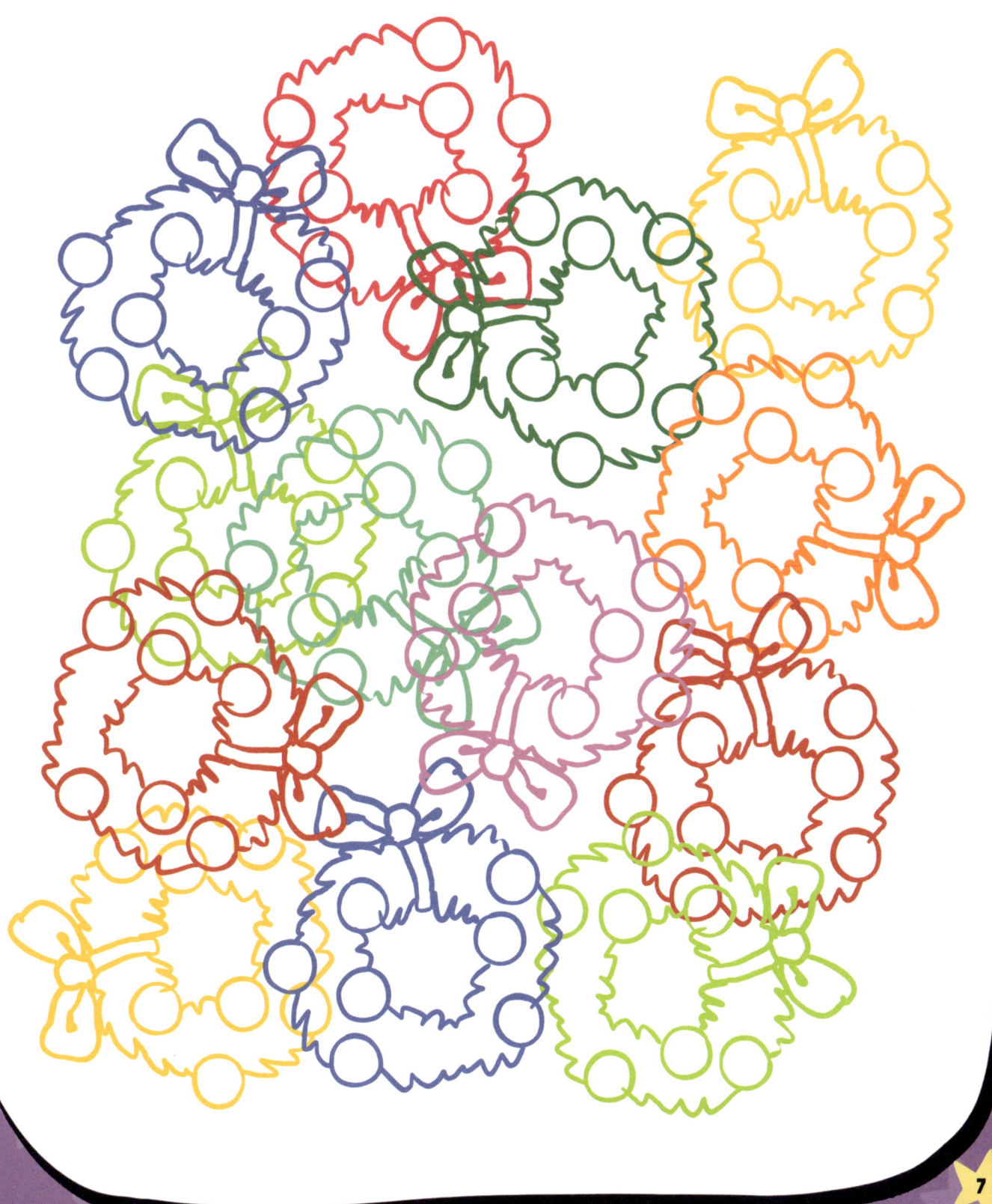

Wrap It Up, Elves!

Can you work out which elf wrapped which gift by matching their outfits to the wrapping paper?

Rockin' Reindeers

Use pencils and pens to complete this festive scene filled with reindeers and holiday cheer.

Puzzle Performance

The elves have sneaked into a very elegant Christmas ballet. Which of the squares below are part of this scene?

A B C D E

Christmas Clusters

Can you find these three groups among the seasonal items below?

North Pole Party

The elves are out celebrating and spreading festive cheer in style! Can you spot the ten differences between these two scenes?

Sleigh Trouble

The elves have tangled up the reindeers' reins! Can you help Santa find which letter leads to the red-nosed reindeer?

Holiday Mix-Up

The elves have lined up some festive treats. Can you spot which group contains all four of these items?

Solo Stocking

All of these stockings have a matching partner, apart from one – can you spot it?

Fix the Sleigh!

Santa needs to leave the North Pole to deliver presents, but his sleigh is in bits! Complete the picture by writing the letters of the smaller pieces in the correct spaces.

A

B

C

D

E

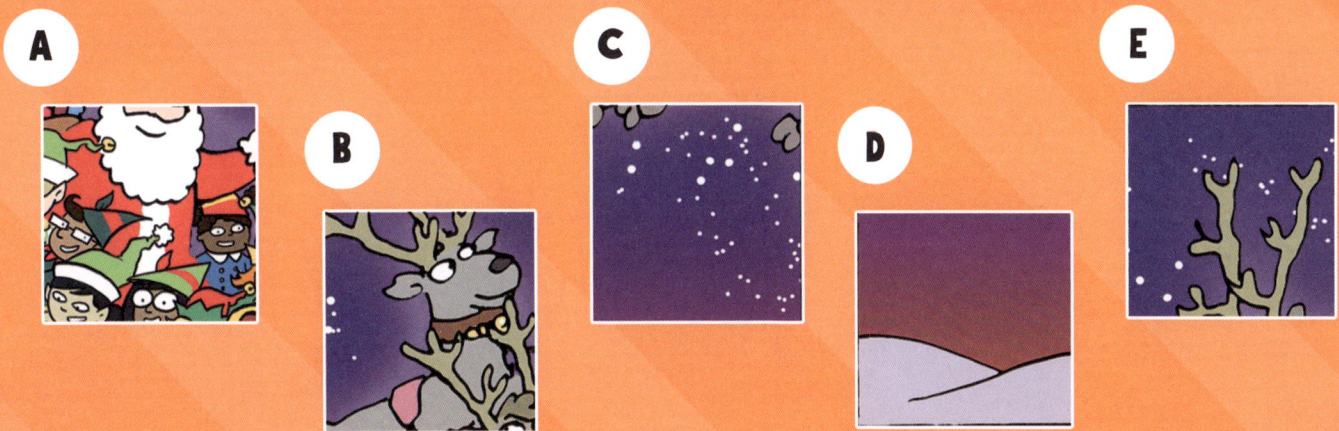

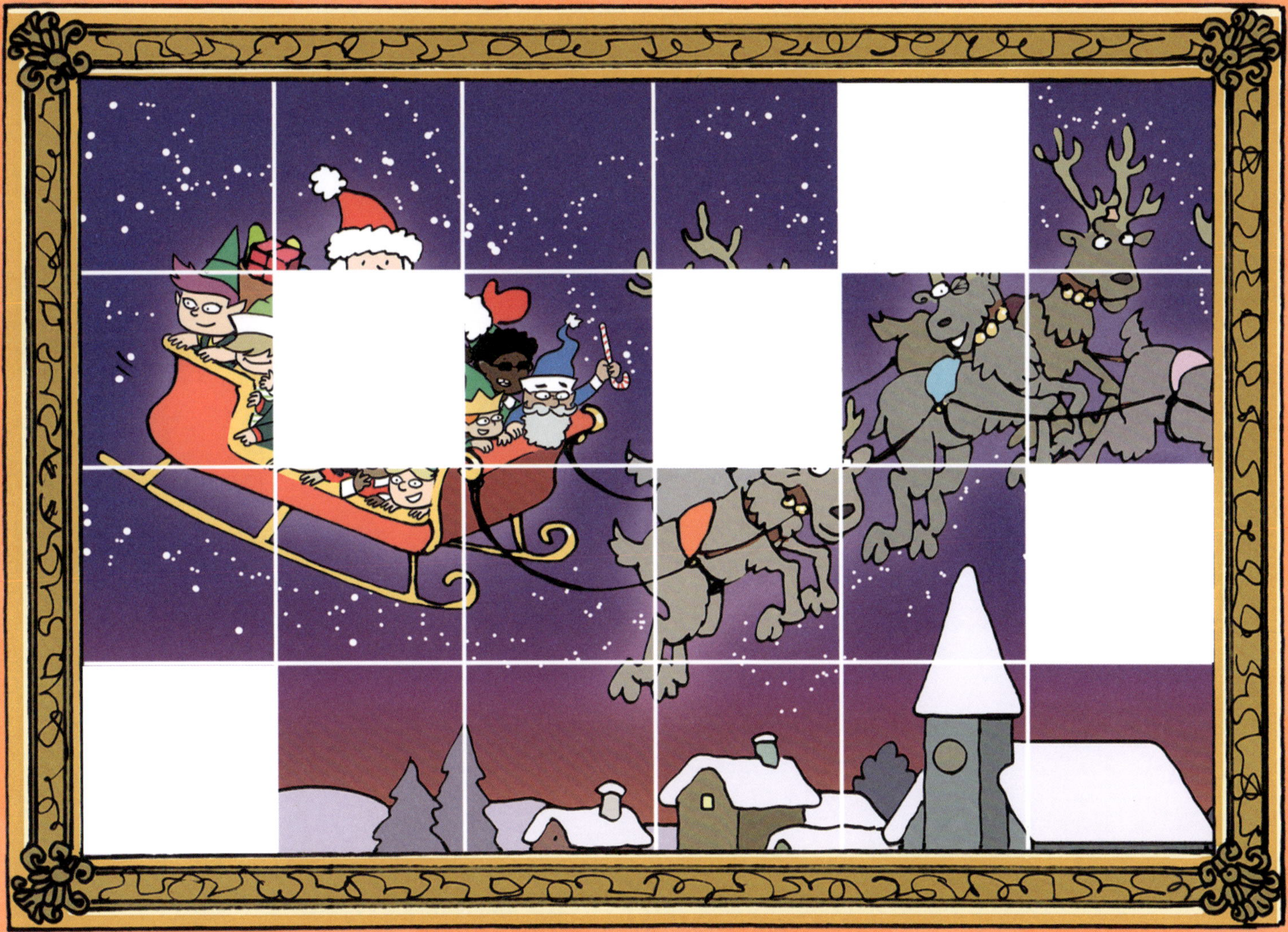

Cookie Theft!

The detectives at Arctic Yard have gathered clues to solve the mystery of who broke into Santa's cookie jar! Can you find the matching elf?

1) I am wearing a green hat.

2) I don't wear glasses.

3) I'm not holding anything in my hands.

Seasonal Sequences

Can you complete each of these rows by working out what belongs in the empty spaces?

Merry Mayhem

This snowy hill is packed with festive skiers ... some gliding gracefully, others tumbling into the snowdrifts! Can you spot the ten differences between these two scenes?

All About Elves

How much do you know about elves? Test your elf knowledge with this quiz. You can find the answers on page 45.

1. What are elves known for making?

    a) Books
    b) Toys
    c) Pizzas
    d) Pottery

2. What do elves wear on their heads?

    a) A baseball cap
    b) A beanie
    c) A pointy hat
    d) A safety helmet

3. What kind of ears do elves have?

    a) Round ears
    b) Long, pointy ears
    c) Folded ears
    d) Floppy ears

4. What activity do they enjoy doing at the North Pole?

    a) Swimming
    b) Sledding
    c) Surfing
    d) Camping

5. Which month is the busiest for elves?

    a) December
    b) January
    c) August
    d) May

Wrap Like An Elf

The elves need your help with some giftwrapping! Decorate this magical present.

Decorations In Disguise

These Christmas trees are looking festive and bright, but something seems a little different! Can you spot the ten merry mismatches in these two images?

Frosty Journey

Can you find a way through this snowflake flurry from start to finish? You can move up, down, left and right but not diagonally. Follow the snowflakes in the order shown at the top.

START

FINISH

Frosty Shadows

Only one of the silhouettes below perfectly matches the snowman. Can you figure out which one?

Oh Tangled Trees!

It's a Christmas tree pile up! How many trees can you find in the jumble below?

Which Elf Should Be Your BFF?

Answer the questions in this flowchart to discover which elf would be your perfect pal.

- Snowman
- Candy canes
- Would you rather build a snowman or make a snow angel?
- Snow angel
- Do you prefer candy canes or chocolate coins?
- Chocolate coins
- It's time to do some Christmas cooking. Would you rather build a gingerbread house or make reindeer cookies?
- Gingerbread house
- Reindeer cookies

You meet up with your friends. Do you sing Christmas carols or watch Christmas films?

Sing carols → **JINGLE!** No party is complete without Jingle and her friends singing songs and making music.

Watch films → **BUDDY!** Buddy loves nothing more than snuggling up on the sofa with a bowl of treats and a Christmas movie.

You finish your homework early. Do you watch a Christmas film or bake Christmas cakes?

Bake cakes → **MAX!** The elf in charge of the treats, Max is never far from the kitchen, handing out sweets and biscuits.

It's snowing outside. Do you run out to throw snowballs or stay inside playing a board game?

Out to the snow! → **FROSTY!** Frosty is the fastest snowball maker there is, and she loves nothing more than a snow day!

Board game → **DASH!** Chief toy maker Dash knows about all the newest toys and games and is always eager for a friend to play with.

It's Christmas Eve. Do you settle down to play a board game with family and friends or do you help prepare for the big day tomorrow?

Prepare for Christmas Day → **HEIDI!** Famous for her present wrapping skills, Heidi loves to make sure everything is ready for Christmas Day.

Elves Down Under

In Australia, Christmas is celebrated with sun, surf and sand, as people enjoy barbecues and beach days. Which of the squares below are part of this scene?

A

B

C

D

E

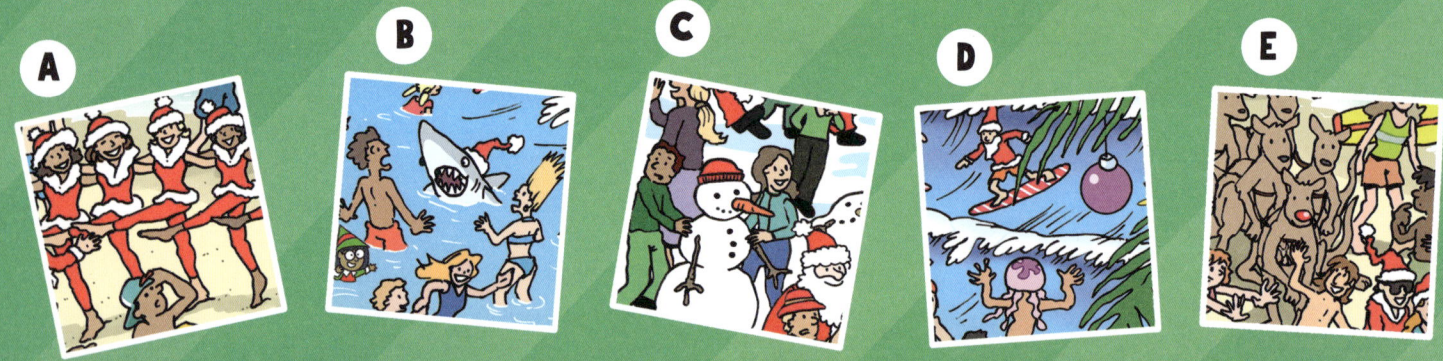

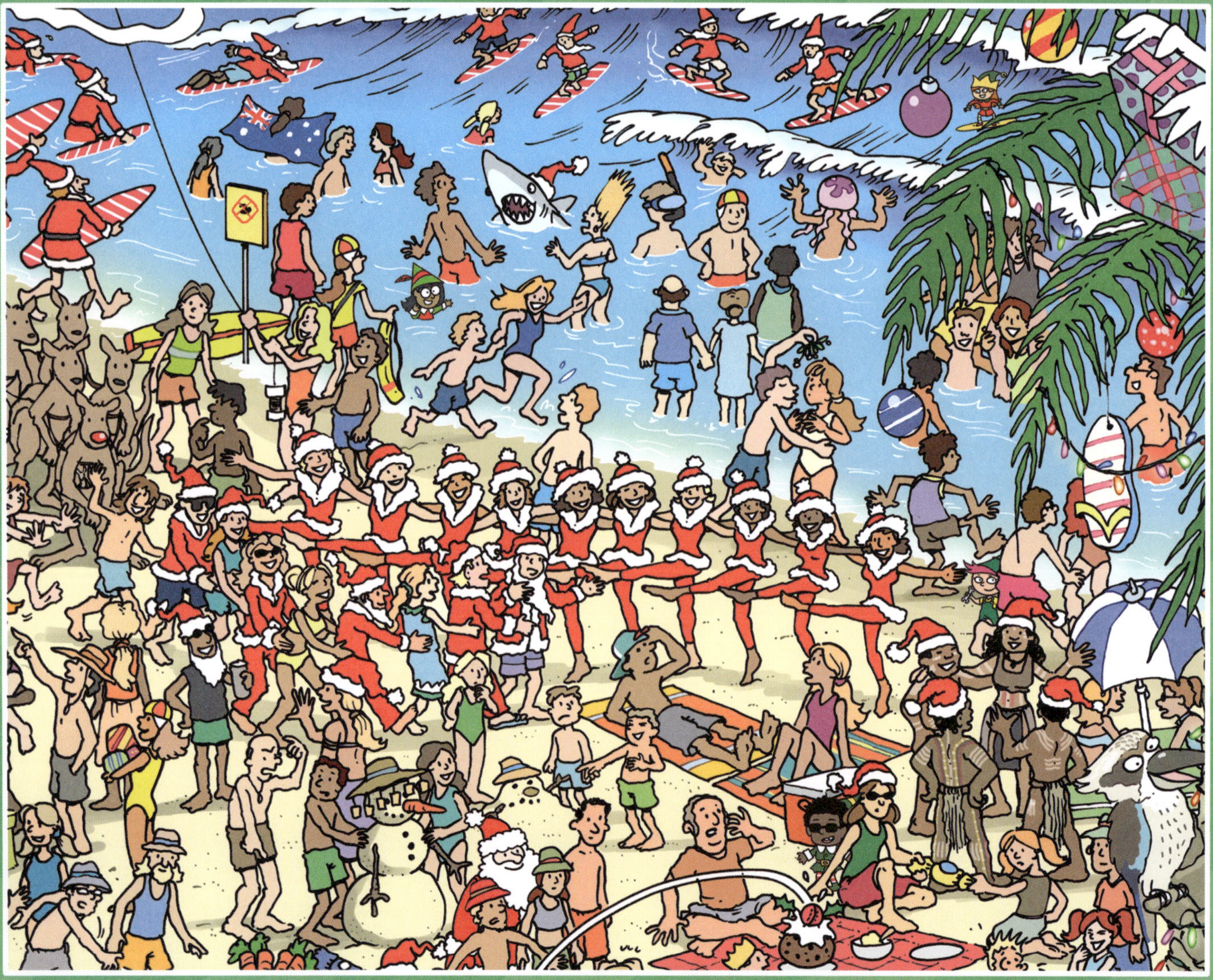

Fireside Fun

While Santa's busy squeezing down the chimney, take a good look at this scene. Turn the page to test your memory with some fun questions!

Fireside Fun Questions

Now that you've studied the scene, see if you can answer these tricky questions.

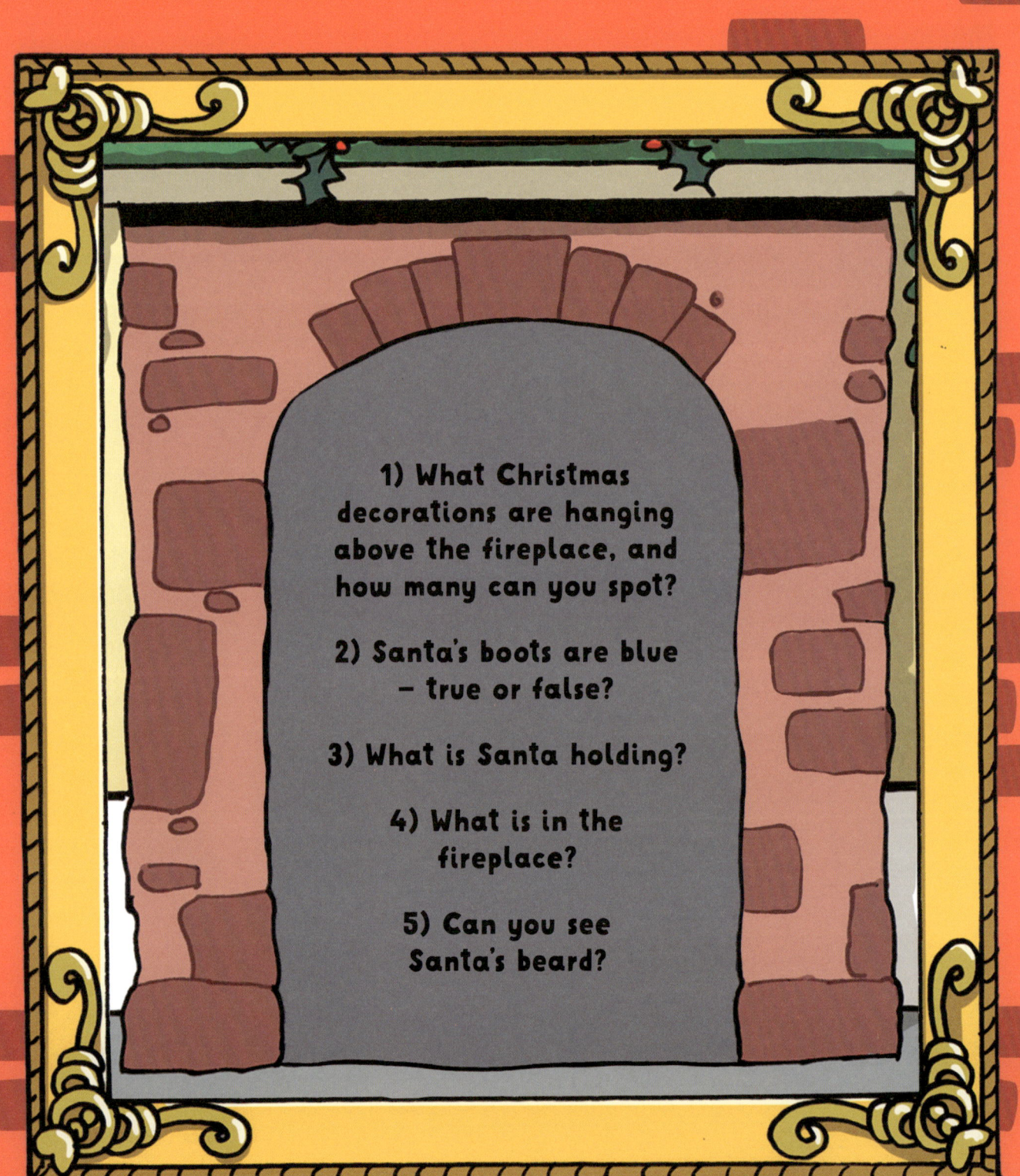

1) What Christmas decorations are hanging above the fireplace, and how many can you spot?

2) Santa's boots are blue – true or false?

3) What is Santa holding?

4) What is in the fireplace?

5) Can you see Santa's beard?

Merry Art

Use pens, pencils or crayons to complete this jolly scene.

All the Answers

Page 6
Silhouette D

Page 7
There are 13 wreaths.

Page 10-11

Page 8

Page 12

Page 14-15

Page 13

Page 16
Letter A leads to Rudolph.

Page 17
Group D has all the items.

Page 18

Page 19

Page 20-21

Page 22

Page 24-25

Page 23

Page 26
1. Toys
2. A pointy hat
3. Long, pointy ears
4. Sledding
5. December

Page 28-29

Page 30

Page 31

Page 32
Silhouette E

Page 33
There are 21 trees.

Page 36

A

B

D

E

Page 37-38

1. There are 4 stockings hanging above the fireplace.
2. False – Santa's boots are black.
3. Santa is holding his present sack.
4. There is a log pile in the fireplace.
5. No, you cannot see Santa's beard.

Page 40-41

Written and edited by Gabriele Del Romano
Design by Moesha Kellaway

Manufacturer: First published in Great Britain in 2025 by Buster Books, an imprint of Michael O'Mara Books Limited, 9 Lion Yard, Tremadoc Road, London SW4 7NQ
www.mombooks.com

Represented by: Authorised Rep Compliance Ltd, Ground Floor, 71 Lower Baggot Street, Dublin D02 P593, Ireland
www.arccompliance.com

W www.mombooks.com/buster
f Buster Books
○ @buster_books

This book contains material previously published in *Where's Santa?*, *Where's the Penguin?* and *Where's the Elf?*

Copyright © Buster Books 2013, 2014, 2018, 2025

All rights reserved. You may not copy, store, distribute, transmit, reproduce or otherwise make available this publication (or any part of it) in any form, or by any means (electronic, digital, optical, mechanical, photocopying, recording, machine readable, text/data mining or otherwise), without the prior written permission of the publisher. Any person who does any unauthorized act in relation to this publication may be liable to criminal prosecution and civil claims for damages.

A CIP catalogue record for this book is available from the British Library.

ISBN: 978-1-83725-071-4

1 3 5 7 9 10 8 6 4 2

This product is made of material from well-managed, FSC®-certified forests and other controlled sources. The manufacturing processes conform to the environmental regulations of the country of origin.

This book was printed in June 2025 by Shenzhen Wing King Tong Paper Products Co. Ltd., Shenzhen, Guangdong, China.

For further information see www.mombooks.com/about/sustainability-climate-focus
Report any safety issues to product.safety@mombooks.com